# The Give Up Queen

Dedicated to all brave girls who never give up

# The Give Up Queen

## By Rachel Klein

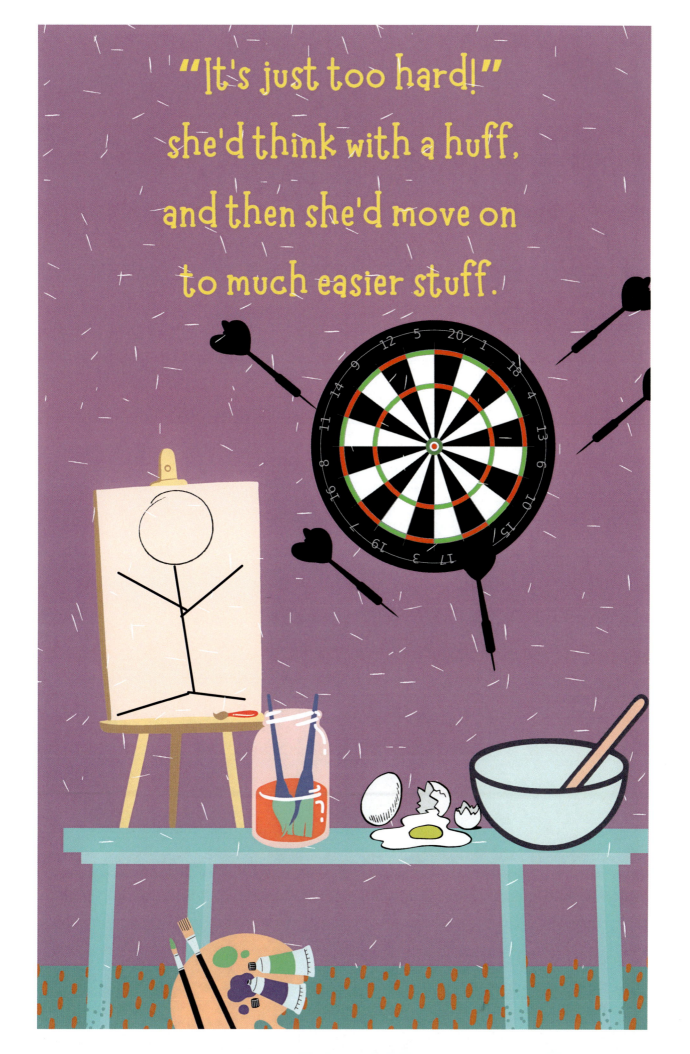
"It's just too hard!" she'd think with a huff, and then she'd move on to much easier stuff.

"Well, never again will I give that a try, I'm just not a baker!" she said with a sigh.

She tried them all once, but they just seemed too tough! She threw each try away and cried, "Enough is enough!"

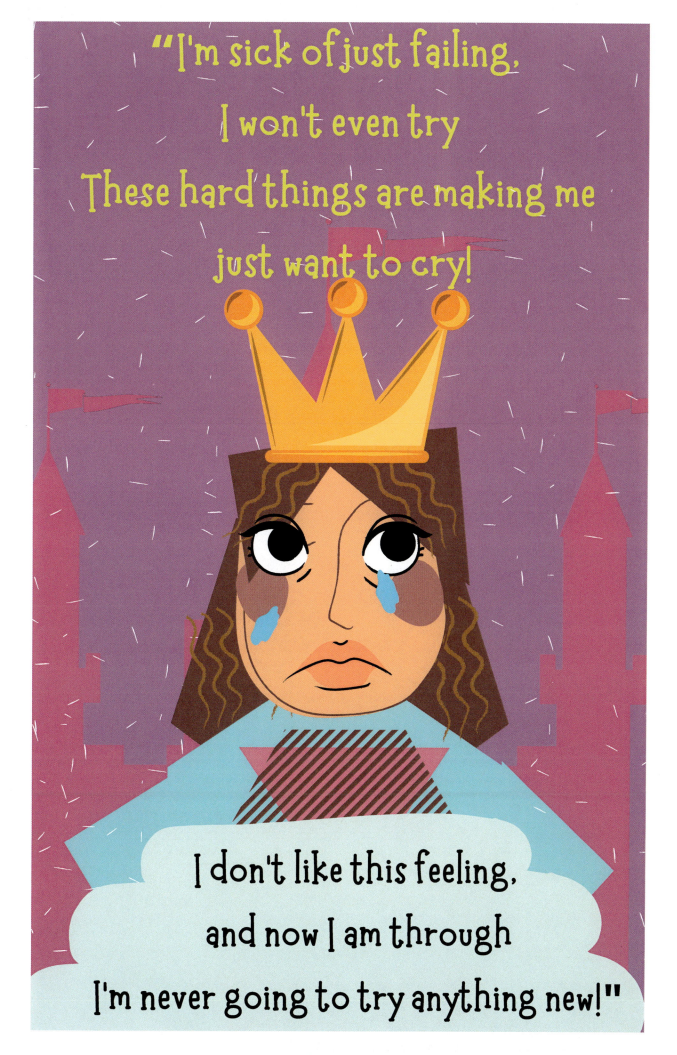

Until one day she was out for a ride
when her horse tripped on a log
and fell on it's side.
She looked around for someone to help
and realized she was out all by herself.

With no one to help her, she felt so alone
and didn't know how
she'd find her way home.
"It's just too hard, I know I can't do it!"
Then she plopped down to think for a minute.

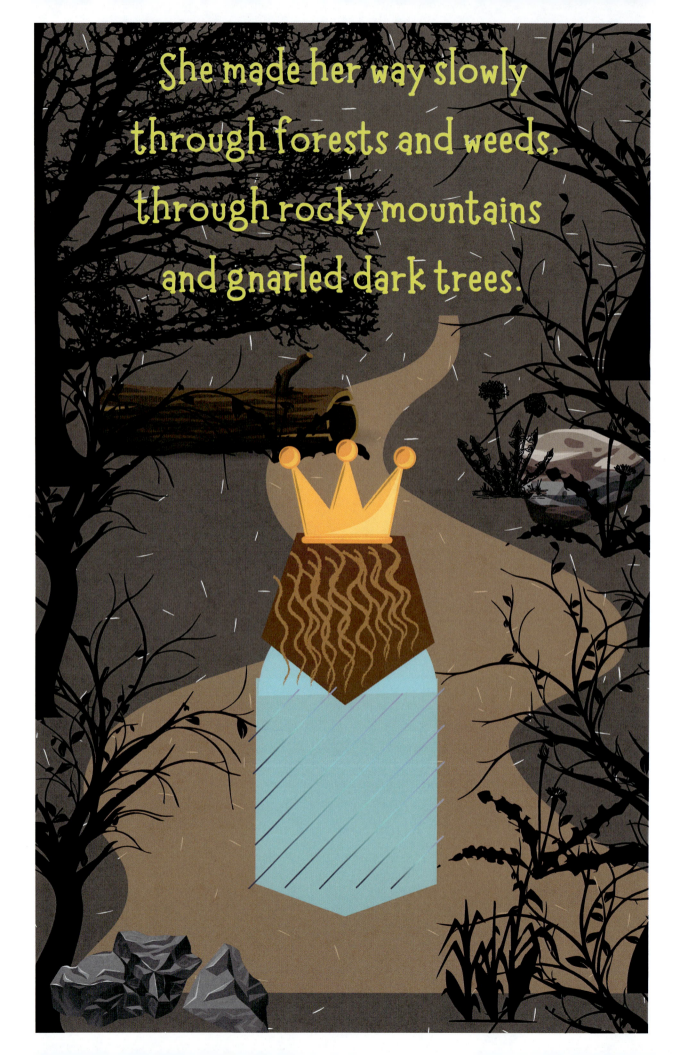

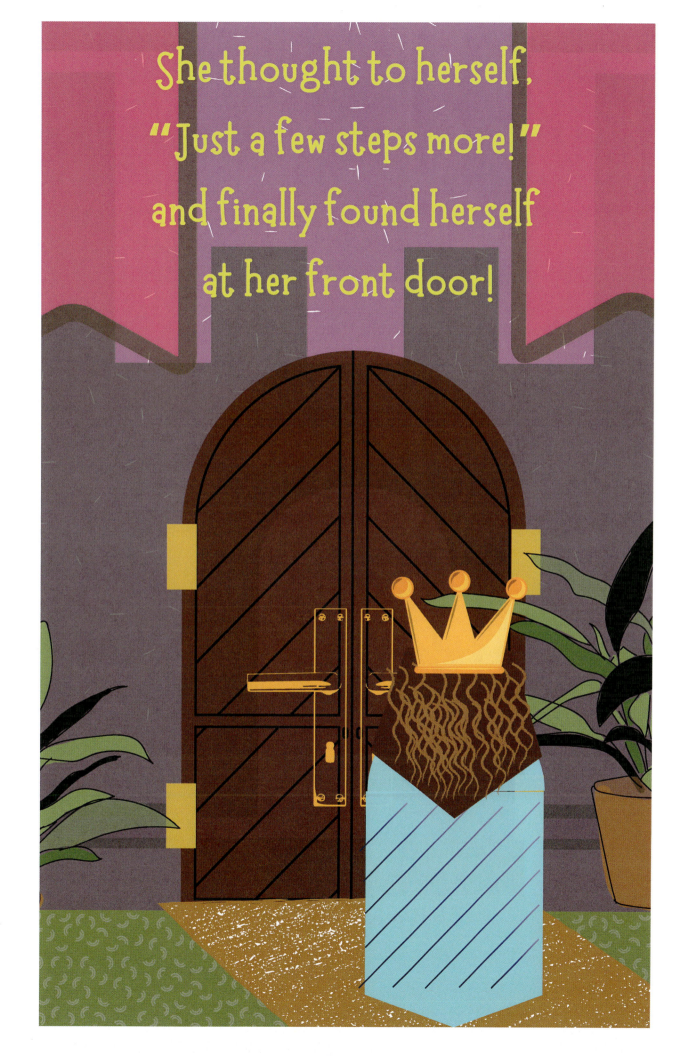

Her parents were there looking concerned
"My daughter, we're happy that you have returned!
But how did you get here?"
they both looked quite shocked.
The Queen just shrugged and said simply
"I walked."

And from that day forth she never gave up.
She knew she was made of much tougher stuff,
Living life is worth giving a try,
you can't just let everything
pass you right by.

So next time you feel like just giving up, remember you're made of much stronger stuff. Keep on persisting when things do get tough, because YOU aren't the Queen of Giving Up!